Where Flowers May Wilt

Brittanie Watts

Published by Brittanie Watts, 2024.

WHERE FLOWERS MAY WILT

First edition. October 18, 2024.

ISBN: 979-8227017420

Written by Brittanie Watts.

This book I dedicate to my loyal supporters. To the ones barely making it in life and yet somehow find the strength to push through. I love all of you! Stay a little longer, love a little harder, and always cherish every moment as if it's the last.

I'm told my body is a temple
But I've been fooled
By false saints
Vandalized
My temple is in array
Because I was led astray

Body to body
Looking for one to keep
Asking the same old question
"Could you be the one?"
Searching high and low
As if love was meant to be
Captured by greed
As if my lust could form love
Out of thin air
Like magic

I've waited long enough for a sign
Prayed to gods I didn't believe in
Screamed at the top of my lungs
Wasted hours pacing
Losing sleep I'll never get back
Mind racing
Time wasting
I'll never understand
How you could just leave
Someone you claimed to love so much
I wasn't even worth a goodbye to you

I watched you leave
No words in your wake
I'm reminded you're not there
With every breath that I take
I'm floating in this illusion
Believing you'll come back to me
Watching the door, waiting for you
Screaming to god not to let it be
Soaking in my madness
Crying in my sadness
Please take this pain away
I cannot bear it to stay

I carry on
With pain that grows
like mold in a basement

You were supposed to be my first example
Of what love was
You made me believe that
The handprints on my skin was what love looked like
You thought it was only skin deep
It was enough to last a lifetime
I have scars you cannot see
And I have words that you will not hear
While I was blocking out
The trauma that you created
You were blocking out your fault in it all
I guess you thought your words were harmless
But you can't explain to me why
They are still stuck in my head
You laugh them off as if you never said them
You are in denial
You made yourself believe a lie
Now you live in your fantasy land
While I have to cope with the reality
Now that I've had to unlearn
All of the trauma I was taught
You want to take credit for the person that I have become
But you cannot take credit for something
That I had to rebuild

Are we just filling
The empty spaces
To pretend that we aren't lonely
The clocks been ticking loud
My ears are growing tired
I just want to rest my head a minute
In your lap of make believe

I waited for you
Like morning dew
You didn't come as freely though
You didn't come at all

You made me believe that my mental struggles
Made me a certain type of person
You put me into a category but never bothered to know me
You created a fantasy for yourself
And spit on me to make yourself feel better
I bet you feel so grand on your false high horse
I bet reality will slap you harder than any words I could ever say
I'm just sad I won't be around to witness your fall from grace

Empty spaces
Empty mind
I'm traveling at full speed ahead
With no sense of time

I hope that when you heal
You do not blame me
Addiction had a stronger hold on you
And I couldn't grip you hard enough
Please don't be mad
That I fell away
I loved you so much
But you loved the way you felt
Drunk or high
More than you loved me
I had to let go
You were destroying yourself
And I was destroying me over you
As if those decisions
Could've been influenced by me
I was tearing myself apart
Thinking I could save you from yourself
Taking all that I had for myself
And throwing it at the wall
Hoping to break through to you
I will always hurt
I will always feel that something is missing
I have a hole in my chest
That you used to live in
I hate myself for letting go
But I had to save myself

I am trapped
With a stranger
Do you not notice
I am not me?
Behind my eyes and smile
I'm at war
This foreign alien
Has taken control of me
I do not recognize myself anymore
These thoughts
These feelings
It's like they aren't mine
I am not me

Your words of love
are like bandaids
And yet I feel as though
I'm supposed to cherish them
As if they're supposed to change everything

The words spilling so fast
I do not agree with them
I know I'll regret them
I look at the bottle of pills
In my hand
Wonder what death would be
If I were to slip into its embrace
I think if I could see the aftermath
I'd cry and laugh
Cry for those who really loved me
But laugh at those who pretend they did
Death is funny like that
When you're gone
Your enemies crawl out like cockroaches
From the corners you forbade them to
And lap for pity like kittens with milk

They have been selling ideas of my body
Long before I had the choice

I've been manic
In a panic
Ready to ruin my life
I've been looking at those pills
Researching what kills
Ready to go
They say suicide isn't the way
But why should I stay

Contorting my body
To fit your image of perfection
Was never in my plan

Being friends with a coward
Is like talking to shadows
That appear solid
It's like talking to yourself
To hear the echo
From some distant cave
Being friends with an addict
Is like watching your life crumble
Except you can't catch the pieces
It's like calling around
Trying to hunt a ghost
when they disappear
Being friends with a liar
Is like touching a rose
And expecting not to get poked
It's like walking in the dark

Grief is weird
How it twists up inside of you
Hides and eats at you
How it unexpectedly bursts free
And washes you in pain all over again
Grief doesn't go away
It finds it's place inside of you
And builds a nest
You find yourself surrounded with it
Unable to escape it's grasp
It's in the trees, in the air that you breathe
Especially in the sky
It's in memories and places
It's in all the spaces
Grief is weird
But it's part of you and it's part of me

I'm jealous
Of the sun
Kissing your skin
I'm jealous
Of the wind
Brushing against you
Of the eyes
That behold you
When mine cannot

I still try
To reach out
My fingers brushing
The air
As if you're a ghost

I want to be happy
But I'm scared to let go
And fall into the unknown
Who am I without my pain
I don't know that I could
Ever be the same
I cling for inspiration
Words sourced from my soul
What happens when I find myself
And I'm whole
Will I then lose my talents
Become some nameless face
Among the crowd
I wish I could keep myself
I wish I were proud
Healing is scary
I've never heard anyone say that

We had silently let go
Neither one of us
Acknowledged the other walking away
Back to back
We drifted further apart
I barely felt your hand slip from mine
Never heard the last words
I'm certain ran through your mind
I'm unsure if you're looking back
Because I am not

Silence
It pounds my eardrums
Until I feel as though I'm losing it
I scream for you to see me
To tell me my time wasn't in vain
To tell me I fucking mattered
But I hear nothing
I want to hate you
I want to curse your name
Until your life crumbles
I want to slam through this wall so hard
That you're forced to look at me
My insides are in turmoil
Full of so much rage and residual love
I don't know whether I'd hug you or punch you
Maybe both
What I do know is that you fucked me up

You were so quiet
I forgot you existed
And for a moment my world was bliss

The day the rain
Smelled of clean earth
The day the wind blew chills
Up the hairs on my arm
Was the day I watched you
Back turned
Leaving my life for good

I light up a cigarette
I haven't smoked in years
To try to forget you
To try to soak up these tears
But I swear
They're tattooed on my face
Etched into my being
I try to hide them with grace
But fail miserably
I think of moving on
It makes me sick to my stomach
All those wars we fought for nothing
You came to bring havoc
And then you left

Morning dew
Dripping from the eaves
How the wind rustles
And blows the leaves
I think of you
In the stillness of the morning
When the birds sing their songs
My heart still aches
My soul still longs
I could lay out in the rain
Drown in all my sorrow
You wouldn't save me
Or lend me a penny to borrow
And yet I yearn for you

Addiction is a thief
It stole my best friend
Drug him away quietly
I didn't even get to say goodbye

I'm in a landslide
Sliding down a slope
Into a dark deep depression
Walls closing in around me
I can't breathe anymore
I'm suffocating silently

The nightmare of losing you
Replays in my head over and over
Until I'm a pool of tears and snot
Such a pitiful illusion I cling to

I felt as though I was the glue
Holding everything together so that it didn't perish
Then I failed
I couldn't keep it together anymore
The pieces fell at my feet
I just watched it all crumble down
A fire burning all around me
All I could do was stand there
In the blink of an eye, the world I had known was gone
Replaced with such an unfamiliar scene of calamity
I blamed myself for not being able to give any more of myself
Oh how I wept when the monument
I had been holding up collapsed
What a bitter end
To something I once thought of as my home

Always a placeholder
Never a place to stay
Filling empty voids of time
Healing broken parts
Giving out pieces of me
To the broken
Until I'm one of them
Guiding the lost
Until I'm lost with them
Like a broken ship I sink
Except no one swims
To rescue me

Loving you
And losing you
Felt the same

Cried all my tears
I just feel numb
I want to crawl into a hole
I am no one
Wish I could relive
Our last moments together
Wish I had told you I loved you
That I wanted to see you get better
But drugs and your new life
Robbed me of that
I would've dropped everything for you
Drove to where you're at
But as is the way of life
You gain and you lose
If I could've kept you the way we promised
If I had a choice, it would be you I chose
Those pictures of you
Burning a hole in my heart
I don't know how to heal
But I know I have to start

Hatred is a heavy burden
So I try to shrug it off
But it's become a second skin
I'm trapped within

Even if you told me
The world was ending tomorrow
Even if you said we'd never make it
Even if you looked at me
With those big blue eyes
Told me you didn't want to see me
Even then
I'd follow you into the unknown

As I sit and ponder
I'm met with grief
Grief for things that cannot come to pass
Grief for things yet to pass
I'm consumed by it
The anxiety surrounding it
As if it was tangible
I smell it, I taste it
I feel it grip my chest so hard
I can't breathe
Like it's trying to suffocate me
Yet I walk on into the known
My feet can't fail me
But I will

Why are waiting rooms
Always a little awkward
The anxiety gripping the wheel
Driving hard and fast
Into a concrete wall
Wanting to leave
But feeling trapped
Like this room is a prison
I'm locked in

My feelings are
Over crowded
Over populated
Overwhelming
I'm over it

Friends with your ghost
We sit and tell stories
About what used to be
What could've been
And what never will be
I can't live without you
So I'll settle
For the ghost of your memory
Oh how it haunts me
Lurking in the background
Of every picture we ever took
Standing at the front
Of every memory I shared with you
I scream as if you could hear me
I cry as if my tears could bring you back
But they're lost
I'm lost
Without you

You didn't ask
But I'm hurting
You couldn't look me in the eye
To say you were sorry
When all I wanted
Was your embrace
You gave me your absence
I feel as though I'm falling
Hopelessly to the bottom
You used to hold my hand
Now I'm grasping at the air
I can't let you go
I'm holding onto the memories
Like my life depends on it

Your loss has consumed me
It's my every thought
My every feeling
I'm breaking apart
Healing
And falling apart all over again

I look for you
In every strangers face
Hoping I pass you again
Hoping I can tell you
What's been on my mind
How it's been clouded
With memories of you
How I've wilted
Without you in my life

I did time
Inside your mind
You say
It rains
All day
And when I think of you
I think of us
Of all sores
And closed doors
When my mind drifts away
I find my peace
Beg it to stay
But it dissipates
Like your love did

I can't find peace
My soul paces
The empty corners
That you used to occupy

Spilled cereal
That's all it took
I cower in your shadow
Waiting for the strike
You are a predator
And I am your prey

Tip toeing
Quiet whispers
Unwilling to disturb you
From your tv coma
My brother shush's me
He's afraid too

Your anger is scorching
Silently filling your eyes
I see it in the firm line of your lips
Smell the whiskey on your breath
I know what is to come
Yet I'm frozen in place

Today I looked
At pictures of us
And the pain split me in two
Grieving a living person
Is a pain I've never known
It's a heartbreak
That doesn't stop
Losing my best friend
Hurts so deep I can't breathe
I feel like I could die
Today I looked
At pictures of us
And I smiled through the tears

I remember the first time
I touched myself
I found pleasure
That snowballed
Into pleasure equals love
I've been searching for love
In the arms of strangers
Wondering why I can't find it
When pleasure never equaled love

My love grows like ivy
Tangled around my heart

I stare at the knife
I ponder my life
If everyone is quick to cut my throat
Why don't I
I can't even see my reflection
My vision is clouded
I take a deep breath
Take another drink
What's it gonna take
To rid my head of these things I think
These people
These places
I'm so sick of it all
They wanna laugh at me
They wanna see me fall

Fuck these people
These places
They'll get their karma
I hope the payback is as big
As big Pharma
Workplace, workspace
Unsafe
Always has to be some drama
Fuck these people
These spaces
I find myself in
Fuck these places
I'm claustrophobic
And the walls are caving in

I'm about to snap
About to lose my mind
I take one look around
Looking for a sign
How did I get here
Why have I stayed
The thoughts naw at me
I'll take them to my grave
The thought hits me
The only way out I feel
I know that's not true
But still
I look down at my hands
Wondering what they're capable of
I want to be down deep
No longer above

You let the things they said
Get inside your head
You let it make you feel
As though you were dead
I can't take it anymore
You were only four
You became what they told you
When you really craved more
I can't look you in the eyes
I only hear your cries
If this is where it ends
I hope your sadness dies

Time crouches over me
Condescending
It's face scrutinizing
Every inch of me
Picking at parts of me
Changing
Time is cruel
We're caught in it's web
Time devours
Time creates
Like a magician
Time is neither
Death nor birth
It is simply a follower
For time stalks us

I danced in the fire
Shed my cloak
Just for you
Your eyes wandered
You couldn't see me
You saw through me
I was just a ghost

Your memory stalks me
Wraps its greedy hands around my throat
I can't breathe

Your essence
Is still trapped in my skin
I try to wash it off
It's too deep within
I can't erase you
From my mind
I thought I was through
Sometimes love is blind
I wish you away
As if that could work
But you're here to stay
I watch you smirk
My pain brings you happiness
You watch me writhe
I succumb to the emptiness
As you just stand by

She was falling in love
Falling apart
Coming together
Going away
All at the same time
She thought she was broken
She was more than whole

You scream
I cower
With anticipation
You're an angry wolf
And I'm your prey
I am trapped
In the den you've created
I wear your anger
I try to cover it up
With long sleeves
And makeup
I smile to pretend
I have to put on a show
Like a never-ending performance
You play along too
I wonder when the monsters
You hide under your bed
Will rip you to shreds
What a relief
Your lack of existence would be

The walls of my mind
Are littered with pictures of you
Somehow it's more painful
Than your presence

I am surrounded with love
But none seeps into my skin
I grasp at the remnants
Trying to take it in
I feel so empty
So numb to the presence
All I want to do is live
But I'm popping antidepressants

Another year
Has passed me by
When I think of you
I still cry
I remember your voice
The way you used to smell
In that house
Your memory dwells
I miss your laugh
How it lit up my world
Your warm smile
I was just a little girl
I visit your grave often
Reminisce about you
I was only ten
But I'll always remember you

I hope I haunt the halls
Of your overcrowded mind
I hope that my memory
Takes your breath away
And not in a good way
I hope you fall in love
With my absence

I want to be close
So close to you
That I don't know
Where you end
And I begin
And I won't care either
I want to be so intertwined
In love with you
I am in love with you
My heart longs
To be one with you

Falling in love
I'm unsure
If it's the birth or death
Of a poet like me

I swim in your blue eyes
Want to drown in your love
I melt in your arms
They're made for me
Your lips made to kiss me
Your body made to fit mine
I am utterly
And completely
Yours

Your hands
Touched me
Not in the way
I want to be touched
I was just a little girl
You told me this was normal
I believed you

The bed is still warm
My arms are empty
I hate that you had to leave
And I'll miss you plenty
But you had to go
You have a life outside of me
I still find myself wishing
A part of that life I could be
Love growing like vines
Tangling around my heart
Please be good I whisper
Please don't tear me apart

The one that got away
I'll write about this
Until the day
My knight comes along
Singing his song

I don't ever feel
Like I'm enough for someone
I look at myself in the mirror
My reflection saying
I don't deserve love
I look at them and wonder
Why anyone would ever want me
I water myself down
Again

You smile
And I melt
Like a snowman
In the Texas sun

To the narcissist
I once loved
You probably think
I can't live without you
That I'm completely
Miserable without you
That I'll break down
And come running back
But the truth is
I'm better off without you
I'm full of the life
That you tried to rob from me
You will always be the villain
In my story
You will never win me back

I cannot help but feel
Your withdrawal
Your losing of interest
In your lack of words
And excitement
My mind confirming
I am not enough
And I never will be

I'd like to believe
That you could be mine
That I could be loved
That I even deserve love

You love my body
For the night
To fill the void
Inside of you
Then discard me
Like used tissue paper
And I let myself
Be used by you
To feel love
To feel wanted
Isn't that what
You wanted?
Me to be yours
For the night
To pretend
That you aren't going
To disappear

I can't ever tell
If my anxiety
Is lying to me
Or if what I feel
Is the truth

Oh how I wish
My body could house you
And be enough
For you to stay
But it never is
Goodbyes stalk me
At every turn
I know that it's only
A matter of time
Until I met them
Face to face

Tears tug at my eyes
I choke them down
Pretend my feelings
Don't exist
Sometimes I wish
I didn't exist

I wake up in a panic
The scars you left
So many years ago
Unseen but very real
Visions of your hand clamped
Over my mouth
Your body pinning mine down
And I'm in hell all over again

I watch these movies
Where the main character falls in love
I cry because I think
Why can't that be me
Am I so unlovable
That I'm doomed
To be alone

You fuck me
I make love to you
And it's not until
It's too late
That I realize
You don't love me
How could you
Love someone
Like me

I know I'm not pretty
Like those other girls
But if you give me a chance
I'll show you the beauty
I house within

I glue
My smile on
But when I walk away
My smile falls
Like broken bridges
Coming apart
Like the fall leaves
Meeting the ground
I crumble inside

You put on an act
A puppet show
I am your puppet
Some grand play
And you're the master
You twist me up
And use me
When you're done
You put me away
For later

House made of glass
You throw stones at my windows
And call it love
But I know better
You don't think I do
So when I walk away
With my broken windows
You should know
There's someone who would
Repair them and admire them

Your sticks and stones
Break my bones
I am not as strong
As you think I am
You know you're wrong
For what you've done
My healing isn't linear
It's twisted and contorted
What I fear
Is that I'll never heal
Back to who I was
That I'll stay disfigured
Just because
I'd be unlovable

I always give too much
Too little
Too soon
Too late
I am a lover
With no lover
A fighter
With no fight
I am alone

I watch you fade
Before me
Your tired eyes
Staring into the abyss
You're soon to join

No goodbyes
No warnings
My heart scattered
I'm in mourning
Memories
That's all you'll be
Wishing our last time together
Had not been so carefree
I wish I knew
What I know now
I'm walking on
Even though I don't know how
I think I'll always love you
But I need to hate
Some would say this was meant to be
As if we sealed our fate

I'm going to forget you
Forget you exist
In my world you're dead
Just smoke and mist
I'll bury you
In an unmarked grave
I'll never visit you
That's what I crave
The banishment of you
Would bring me peace
You don't deserve one ounce of me
Not even a fucking piece
I'll let you rot
In your own pool of misery
I hope you stay there
But I won't be around to see

I wish you away
But in my head you stay
I look up to the sky
Pretend there's a god and pray

Your hand covers my mouth
Calloused by the wars you fight in your head
I smell your hate
And feel your violence tremble through your palms
A deep fear for my life burns through my veins
And I catch on fire
I become riddled with anger
Lashing out with the hate you've infected me with
I want to scream but I am silenced
By your guns pointed to my head
I want to fight but I am pinned down
By your knees against my throat
I can't breathe the toxic you radiate
I choke on the words you use to slit my throat
I suffocate on the hate that you wrap around my neck
You tied a noose and said that it was your love
Your words a noose, every syllable a knot
I just want everyone to know how hard I fought
You took my joy without a second thought
The blistering pain inside me just wants you to rot

When the lightening strikes
I wonder if it struck as hard
As your words did my heart
I wonder if I danced around in the rain
Would it wash me clean of them

I'm the woman that men visit
Like on a vacation
They never stay

I'm the woman that men visit
Like on a vacation
They never stay

You were like a hurricane
A beautiful disastrous being
You swept me away
I believed we'd be one
But as hurricanes always do
You ripped me apart
And abandoned me

I've lost myself crying
Over someone
Who probably never had
Second thoughts about me

You're so caught up in
Feeling nothing at all
That you neglect the idea
That the people around you do

It's sad how time
Tries to erase your smile
I can't exactly remember
How you laughed
I wish I could hear it again
I wish I could hug you
And smell you again
All of these things
I can't have
I am selfish
You are at rest
And I want you back
I didn't have enough time
With you

I have a bone to pick with death
He took so much that I loved
Sometimes it's hard to look around
And love what I have
I get swallowed up in my grief
Overwhelmed with loss

Flowers bloom from the
concrete of my grief
I try to put myself in your shoes
I'm sure you felt relief
This world wasn't good enough
For you to stay here on earth
I wave goodbye as you depart
Off to your rebirth

About the Author

I have struggled with severe depression and anxiety for many years. When I was only 8 years old, I started to write about my pain through poetry. I struggled with self harm and a few attempts at suicide which thankfully were not sucessful as I would not be here sharing with you my most intimate thoughts. I've lived through a lot and I've experienced a lot. I have not yet been able to write about some of the things I've experienced but I hope to gain the courage from my readers to do so.

9 798227 017420